crafty
girl™

accessories

D0592413

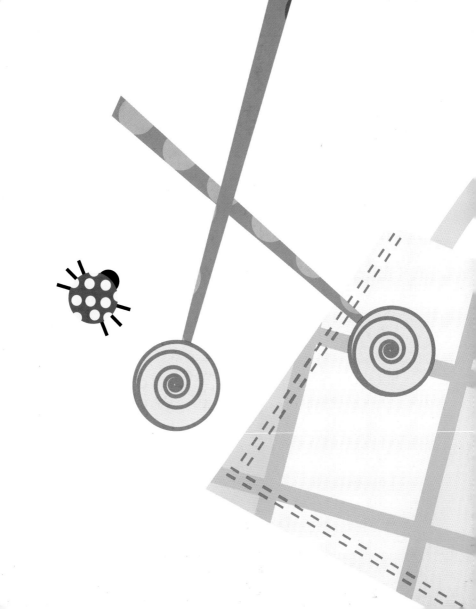

accessories

things to make and do

by Jennifer Traig

CHRONICLE BOOKS

SAN FRANCISCO

Copyright © 2002 by Chronicle Books LLC.
Line drawings copyright © 2002 by Stephanie Sadler.
All rights reserved. No part of this book may be reproduced
in any form without written permission from the publisher.

Library of Congress Cataloging-in-Publication Data:
Traig, Jennifer.
Accessories : things to make and do / by Jennifer Traig.
   p. cm. – (Crafty girl)
   ISBN 0-8118-3151-5
        1. Handicraft for girls—Juvenile literature. 2. Girls' clothing—
Juvenile literature. 3. Dress accessories—Juvenile literature. I. Title.

Printed in Singapore

Line drawings by Stephanie Sadler
Designed and illustrated by Gayle Steinbeigle, Protopod Design

Distributed in Canada by Raincoast Books
9050 Shaughnessy Street
Vancouver, British Columbia V6P 6E5

10 9 8 7 6 5 4 3 2 1

Chronicle Books LLC
85 Second Street
San Francisco, California 94105
www.chroniclebooks.com

Crafty Girl™ is a registered trademark of Chronicle Books LLC.

**Notice: This book is intended as a practical guide to the crafting of accessories.
As with any craft project, it is important that all the instructions are followed
carefully, as failure to do so could result in injury. Every effort has been made to
present the information in this book in a clear, complete, and accurate manner;
however, not every situation can be anticipated and there can be no substitute for
common sense. Check product labels, for example, to make sure that the materials
you use are safe and nontoxic. Be careful when handling dangerous objects. The
author and Chronicle Books LLC disclaim any and all liability resulting from injuries or
damage caused during the production or use of the crafts discussed in this book.**

Aleene's Tacky Glue is a registered trademark of Aleene's Licensing Company, LLC. Astroturf is a regis-
tered trademark of Southwest Recreational Industries, Inc. Ceramcoat is a registered trademark of
Delta Technical Coatings, Inc. Fimo is a registered trademark of Eberhard Faber G.M.B.H. Lucite is a
registered trademark of ICI Acrylics Inc. Mod Podge is a registered trademark of Plaid Enterprises, Inc.
Pee-Chee is a registered trademark of the Mead Corporation. Scotch Tape is a registered trademark of
Minnesota Mining and Manufacturing Company. Styrofoam is a registered trademark of the Dow Chemical
Company. X-acto is a registered trademark of X-acto Crescent Products, Inc.

acknowledgments

Catwalk kisses to my parents, Alain and Judy, for being seen with me even when I dress funny; to my sister Victoria for dressing funny too; to Peter McGrath, Dan McGrath, Wendy McGrath, and Maureen Neff for serving as fashion advisors and role models; to Miriam and Mitzi Schleicher for their fashion 411; to Tali Koushmaro for her crafty fashion ideas; to Angela Hernandez and Daniel Archer for shopping with me; and to Ryan Gray for doing my laundry. A big black-tie thank-you goes to Mikyla Bruder and Jodi Davis for being superlative editors and snappy dressers to boot. And finally, Vidal Sassoon–style thanks to Stephanie Sadler and Gayle Steinbeigle for making this look good.

table of contents

8

There's something special about you. Sure, you look better than everyone else—that's a given. But it's more than that. You've got a sixth sense, and it's *fashion* sense. You can't look at your friends without thinking, "I could fix you *up*." You can't go to the mall without thinking, "I could make this stuff—and I could make it better." You've got a gift, and you want to share it with the world. You want to teach everyone that anything looks better with a couple of sequins and some fun-fur trim, that fleece is truly a miracle fabric, and that accessories make the outfit. In short, it's your destiny to make the world a more fashionable place. *Crafty Girl: Accessories* believes in your mission, and we're here to help with a closetful of hip and happening style ideas. The projects are easy enough for beginners and the sewing-impaired. So all you wallflowers, get ready to bloom.

It doesn't matter what your style is. Maybe your look is futuristic fashion-forward. Maybe you fell off the retro tree and hit every branch on the way down. Maybe you're sporty, or preppy, or hippie, or hip hop. Whether you're a Drama Diva or a Clean Teen, a Rockabilly Betty or a Mall Doll, *Crafty Girl: Accessories* wants to help you make your look look even better. Because for you, it's not really fashion unless you've fashioned it yourself. Off the rack? Perish the thought. Who wants to look like everyone else? Buying is boring. It's also expensive. You'll save stacks of cash by stitching on your own beads, baubles, and butterflies. And you'll get more wear out of the things you already have. Instead of replacing your wardrobe every season, you can update pieces with a nip, a tuck, and a little trim. Even if you end up spending most of your allowance on craft supplies, it's worth it to create a totally unique look.

Making your own fashions ensures that you get exactly what you want, even if what you want is, uh, a little weird.

Speaking of which, we'll admit that being too unique isn't always a good thing. There's a reason you can't find safety-orange quilted palazzo pants in the stores, and the reason is they look really, really awful. Some fashion experiments may fail. That's just part of the process. But in the end, you'll learn a lot about creating a fabulous custom look for yourself. So be brave, be creative, and craft on.

You know that Crafty Fashion is not just for special occasions. You want to dress up the everyday, and projects like the Tough Cuff (page 16) and French Twist Bonbon Hairsticks (page 22) will help you do just that. Later, when the stars come out, you'll really sparkle with a Disco Diva Collar Necklace (page 38) or a Rhinestone Cowboy Belt (page 40). When it's time for bed, don your Glammy Jammies (page 47) and your Tinkerbell Slippers (page 52), and dream of future fashion creations. The next day you can stretch out on a chaise longue and whip up a Milkmaid Kerchief (page 104) without even breaking a sweat. You have only boring, solid-colored fabric on hand? Fret not. Use some fabric paint and the stencils at the back of the book to make your very own, very patterned fabric. If school is in session, transform your locker into a Locker Lounge (page 89) to store your Fancy Folders (page 94) and Bohemian Backpack (page 92). Then march to the head of the class in your Picture Platform shoes (page 81). You're too cool for school. But you're never too busy to look great. So craft an easy, fleecy Rapid Wrap (page 100) in a snap. Then grab your Happy-Go-Lucky Messenger Bag (page 105) and hit the ground running in Chic Sneaks (page 107). You'll go from fashion zero to fashion hero in no time flat.

So let's get started! Use these projects as inspiration, and embellish in any way you see fit. Your first stop is the craft store. There you'll find all the raw materials for your one-of-a-kind creation, from basic supplies like glue and contact paper to more fanciful findings like mini pom-poms and marabou boa. Next, you'll want to hit the bead store to pick up some rhinestones and sequins. Fabric stores are great for fun fur, ribbon, and rickrack trim. Thrift shops have loads of recyclable goodies you can't get anywhere else. You can transform that sad, simple sweater into a truly gorgeous garment with the help of some Glamour Boa Cuffs & Collars (page 36). And that lovely tropical-print tablecloth would make an even lovelier South Seas Sarong (page 58). So comb garage sales, grandma's attic, your own closet—you never know where you'll find fashion inspiration. A Crafty Girl is always on the lookout, so keep your peepers peeled and see what you come up with.

Bear in mind, though, that fashion is serious business, and people can get hurt. Some guidelines: If it's hot (an iron, a glue gun) or sharp (an X-acto knife, wire cutters, a sewing machine), don't use it without adult supervision. Take care, no matter what you're doing. Injuries are never stylish, even if you conceal them with beautifully hand-decorated Band-Aids. And never, ever pair black with navy. You'll hurt your eyeballs and offend our fashion sensibilities.

Other than that, anything goes. So what are you waiting for? Accessorize, accessorize, accessorize!

part 1
everyday
essentials

tough cuff

You will need:

2½-by-8-inch piece of leather, vinyl, or heavy fabric like denim (or just cut a cuff off a sweatshirt)

Pinking shears (if using fabric)

Heavy-duty snap tool (available at fabric and craft stores)

3 heavy-duty snaps (available at fabric and craft stores)

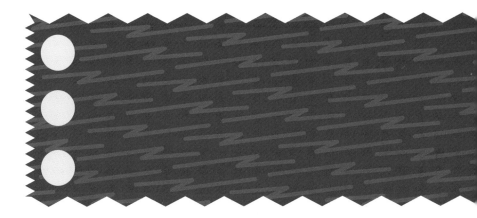

[1] If you're using fabric to make your cuff,
cut the edges of the fabric with pinking
shears to prevent fraying. Otherwise,
skip to Step 2.

[2] Using your snap tool, follow manufacturer's
directions to attach snaps to cuff ends,
spacing them about 1/2 inch apart or so.

[3] Snap on. Snap off. That wasn't so tough, was it?

lost-generation

necklace

Are your orphaned earrings lonesome? Bring all your single earrings together to make a unique necklace. Pearl Drop, meet Ruby Pendant. Opal Marquise, meet Emerald Cluster. It's like a jewelry social, and all the wallflowers are dancing. This project makes a great Mother's Day gift. Once she sees how great they all look together, Mom is bound to forgive you for losing their partners in the first place.

You will need:

Wire cutters and an adult to supervise

Single dangly earrings (save single stud earrings for another project)

Tigertail (coated nylon wire, available by the spool in craft and bead stores)

2 or more crimp beads (little squinchy metal beads that hold things in place, available in craft and bead stores)

Hook-and-eye clasp

Hard-nose pliers (a jewelry tool used for smashing and crimping things together, available in craft and bead stores)

An assortment of beads

[1] Use wire cutters to snip earring hooks off earrings. Be sure to cut just the hook, leaving the dangly part and its loop intact.

[2] Use cutters to cut the length of tigertail you want. About 25 inches should do it, but you can make it longer or shorter. Thread a crimp bead and the hook of your clasp onto one end of the tigertail. Bring tigertail back through crimp bead, pull tight, and pinch crimp bead with pliers.

[3] String your beads and your dangly earrings onto tigertail in the order you want them. You can let them all run together, or you can space them an inch or so apart by pinching a crimp bead on either side of each grouping of beads to keep them in place. When your necklace is long enough, string on a crimp bead and the eye of your clasp. Bring tigertail back through crimp bead, pull tight, and pinch crimp bead with pliers. Use wire cutters to trim excess tail.

[4] Give your fabulous creation to Mom, and promise never to borrow it without asking.

daisy chain

Crazy for daisies? This simple project is for you. String seed beads into an easy, pretty pattern. Will you make a necklace, a bracelet, an anklet, or a belly chain? Better make all four. There's no such thing as too much flower power.

You will need:

Beading thread

Beading needle

Seed beads in at least three colors: one for stems (you'll need lots of these), another for petals (about half as many), and another for centers (not so much)

Hook-and-eye clasp

Scissors

Clear nail polish

[1] Thread a length of beading thread on needle. Thread on a seed bead and position it 6 inches from the end of the thread, so you'll have a 6-inch tail. Take needle back through seed bead to knot.

2 String on 12 stem-color beads and 6 petal-color beads. To make flower shape, take needle back through first petal bead. Next, string on a center-color bead and go out through the fourth petal bead. See diagrams below.

3 Repeat Step 2 until your chain is the desired length.

4 When chain is long enough, take needle through the last seed bead twice to secure. Thread clasp to each end and knot several times to secure. Use scissors to snip away excess thread. Brush knots with clear nail polish for extra strength.

french twist bonbon
hairsticks

Ma chérie, your French twist updo is très jolie, but those bobby pins you're securing it with aren't very interessant. Alors, make these hair-stiques instead. They are fantastique! Adorned with little bonbons, they look good enough to eat, non?

You will need:

Oven-bake polymer clay, like Fimo

2 white plastic sticks, approximately 6 inches long (use lollipop sticks, swizzle sticks or stirrers, chopsticks, or whatever you can find)

Good craft glue, such as Aleene's Tacky Glue

1. Knead polymer clay and shape into two pieces of candy. Make chocolate kisses, peppermints, sour balls, petit fours, lollipops (especially cool if you swirl together a couple different colors by kneading them until the colors are marbled, but not completely mixed), or whatever you like. Using a plastic stick, make a small indentation, 1/4 to 1/2 inch deep, in the bottom of each candy creation. Bake according to package directions. Allow to cool.

2. Dab glue on the end of each plastic stick. Insert sticks into the indentations you made earlier. Allow glue to set.

3. Sweep your hair into a glamorous French twist and secure with *les* hairsticks. *Ooh là là!*

rapunzel hat

Is your 'do a don't? Even Crafty Girls have bad hair days. And all the Crafty Ingenuity in the world won't help a cowlick. You can hang a Christmas ornament on it, hot-glue rhinestones to it, or arrange dried flowers around it, but you're not fooling anyone. Better craft this hat instead. It's adorned with pigtails that behave the way you want when your own hair won't.

You will need:

Scissors

180 feet worsted or sport-weight yarn

Big needle (look for a tapestry needle or a yarn needle)

Knit cap in the same color as your yarn (If you're really crafty, knit your own. Otherwise, store-bought will do.)

[1] Cut yarn into 60 pieces, each 1 yard long.

2 Thread needle with a piece of yarn. Pull strand of yarn through hat, at a point 3 inches or so from the crown. Even up ends of strand so they hang at the same length. Attach 29 more yarn strands in the same place. Braid this bunch of yarn. Secure ends by wrapping a small piece of yarn around them several times and knotting securely.

3 Repeat Step 2 on other side of hat.

4 Tuck your hair under the hat and style your yarn braids any way you like. Wear them down, in chignons, or looped up Heidi-style. Or, if you get really bored, snake pipe cleaners into your braids and go for a Pippi Longstocking look.

matisse scarf

Let's face it: when it's cold outside, fashion takes a backseat.
If it's warm and woolly, we'll wear it, no matter how dull
or dumpy it is. Long johns? Yes. Goofy-looking hat? Sure.
Crusty mittens with a hole in the thumb? Bring it on. Well,
be drab no more, my frosty friend. Fight the winter doldrums
with this easy, fleecy, Matisse-y scarf. It's adorned with
colorful cutouts that resemble abstract masterpieces. Looking
great is an art.

You will need:

¾ yard fleece

Scissors

Needle and thread or sewing machine

Fleece scraps in several contrasting colors

Fabric glue (optional)

[1] First, you'll make the scarf itself. Cut the big
piece of fleece in half lengthwise, so you have
two long strips. Using good old needle and
thread or a sewing machine, sew these two
strips together to make one really long strip.

[2] Next, you'll cut out some decorative shapes from your scraps of fleece. Cut out Matisse-inspired flowers, stars, suns, figures, or letters.

[3] Attach cutouts to your scarf using needle and thread or fabric glue.

[4] All done! Wrap your masterpiece around your neck and consider charging people admission to look at it.

kitten mittens

A Crafty Kitty like yourself knows how to stay warm and fashionable at the same time. You adorn your mittens with cat-inspired fun fur. Purrrrrfect.

You will need:

Measuring tape

Mittens or gloves

Scissors

½ yard fun-fur trim (look for leopard spots, tiger stripes, or fluffy white Persian)

Straight pins

Needle and thread or fabric glue

[1] Measure the circumference of the cuffs of your mittens or gloves and cut two pieces of fun-fur trim to the same length. Make sure the cuffs of the mittens or gloves are roomy enough to slip your hand in without stretching them too much. Once the trim is stitched on, they won't be very stretchy.

2. Secure trim to cuffs with straight pins, then sew in place with needle and thread. Remove pins. If you're in a big rush, simply affix trim with fabric glue, and allow to set.

3. All done! Just pull them onto your paws. *Meow.*

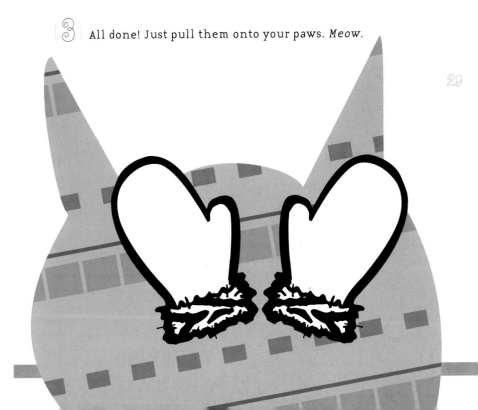

creature clips

Bugs and food in your hair? It's not bad hygiene; it's wacky Crafty Fashion. All it takes are some plastic creatures and store-bought clips for totally unique hair accessories.

You will need:

Good craft glue, such as Aleene's Tacky Glue

Plastic bug, butterfly, fish, sushi, candy, mini pom-pom, or whatever you like

Hair clip (the plainer, the better)

[1] Glue creature to clip.

[2] Allow glue to set. That's it! Make a whole swarm.

journal jackets

It doesn't seem fair that you get to wear adorable jackets and your journal doesn't. Perhaps you should make it a fashionable little coat. Here are some ideas to get you started.

You will need:

Measuring tape

Journal

Scissors

Cover material, such as fun fur, Astroturf, felt, or vinyl

Good craft glue, such as Aleene's Tacky Glue

Decorations: googly eyeballs, mini pom-poms, silk or plastic flowers, rickrack, ribbon, buttons, felt cutouts, plastic food, plastic creatures, silk butterflies, rhinestones, beads, pearls, sequins, or whatever you like

continued on next page

[1] Measure your journal from back to front and top to bottom, and cut your cover material to fit. For example, for a 5-by-7-inch journal with a 1-inch-thick spine you'd need an 11-by-7-inch piece of cover material.

[2] Glue cover material to journal and allow to set. Now for the decorating. Some ideas:

- Cover journal with fun fur, then glue on googly eyes and a pom-pom nose.
- Cover journal with Astroturf. Glue on silk or plastic flowers.
- Cover journal with felt. Glue on rickrack or ribbon. Then decorate with buttons or felt cutouts of stars, hearts, flowers, or whatever you like. Use the stencils at the back of the book.
- Cover journal with checkered tablecloth vinyl. Glue on miniature plastic food and ants.
- Cover journal with flowered vinyl. Glue on silk butterflies and plastic bugs.
- Cut a frame from fun-fur, felt, or vinyl. Glue three sides of frame to journal cover, leaving one side unattached so you can slip in a picture of your favorite person.
- Skip the cover material and glue rhinestones, beads, pearls, and sequins all over.

[3] When glue is dry, write an entry about how crafty you are.

part 2
nightlife necessities

glamour boa

cuffs & collars

Plain sveaters are just so boring, sveetheart. You must glam them up vith fluffy boa trim. It's so easy you von't even need the vardrobe girl to do it for you. Vonce you get started, you'll vant to sew boa on everything in your closet. Don't you just lufffff fluffy feathers? Vonderful, dahhhling!

You will need:

Measuring tape

Sweater or whatever you want to update

Scissors

Marabou boa

Straight pins

Needle and thread

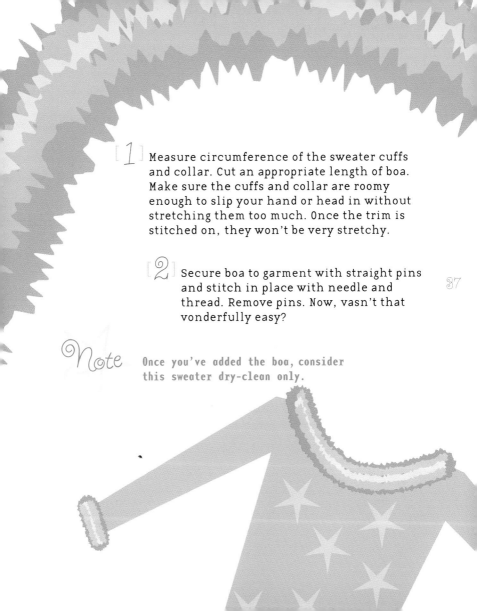

[1] Measure circumference of the sweater cuffs and collar. Cut an appropriate length of boa. Make sure the cuffs and collar are roomy enough to slip your hand or head in without stretching them too much. Once the trim is stitched on, they won't be very stretchy.

[2] Secure boa to garment with straight pins and stitch in place with needle and thread. Remove pins. Now, vasn't that vonderfully easy?

Note Once you've added the boa, consider this sweater dry-clean only.

disco diva

collar necklace

Looking for a necklace with sizzling '70s style? We've got a hot little number for you. This bold gold collar would have gotten you past the velvet rope at Studio 54 for sure. The best part: It's easier than the Electric Slide and you can whip it up in less time than it takes to sing a chorus of "Disco Inferno."

You will need:

Wire cutters and an adult to supervise

15½-inch gold link chain

Gold wire neck ring (available at craft and bead stores)

10 gold beads

1   Using your wire cutters, cut gold chain into 9 pieces. You'll need two 1½-inch pieces; two 1⅝-inch pieces; two 1¾-inch pieces; two 1⅞-inch pieces; and one 2-inch piece.

2 Thread onto your neck ring a gold bead, a 1½-inch piece of chain, another bead, a 1⅝-inch piece of chain, another bead, a 1¾-inch piece of chain, another bead, a 1⅞-inch piece of chain, another bead, the 2-inch piece of chain, another bead, a 1⅞-inch piece of chain, another bead, a 1¾-inch piece of chain, another bead, a 1⅝-inch piece of chain, another bead, a 1½-inch piece of chain, and another bead.

3 Put on your satin jeans, your Halston halter, and your hot Disco Diva Collar Necklace and hit the dance floor. Burn, baby, burn.

rhinestone
cowboy belt

You're a little bit country, and a little bit rock 'n' roll. This beaut of a belt lets you be both in high style. It's rodeo and Rodeo Drive. It'll look great at the Grammies, no matter what category you're nominated in. Rock on!

You will need:

Dressmaker's chalk pencil

Leather belt, 1½ to 2 inches wide

Good craft glue, such as Aleene's Tacky Glue

Flat-back rhinestones

[1] First, decide what you want your belt to say: "Rock Star," "Princess," "Sweetheart," "Red Hot," "Cowgirl," "Rodeo Queen," "Crafty Mama," or your name. Write the words lightly in chalk pencil on your belt.

[2] Glue rhinestones onto the letters. If you like, you can glue more rhinestones onto the buckle for a touch of Elvis-style flash. Allow to set.

[3] Write a country-rock ditty about how cute your belt is.

floating

sparklers

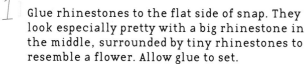

Snow and mist look so pretty in your hair—like, for one second. But then the moisture makes the frizzies come out, and your bangs get all flat, and no amount of gel in the world is going to help you. Mother Nature can be so cruel. Now you can get the pretty effect without the yucky wetness with these sparkly hair accessories. Rhinestones float magically in your hair like dewdrops.

You will need:

Good craft glue, such as Aleene's Tacky Glue

Flat-back rhinestones

Snaps

1 Glue rhinestones to the flat side of snap. They look especially pretty with a big rhinestone in the middle, surrounded by tiny rhinestones to resemble a flower. Allow glue to set.

2 Snap onto hair strands. Scatter throughout loose, waved hair for a dewdrop effect.

sparkle twisties

Who knew ordinary trash twisties could become high-fashion hair ornaments? A little glitter, a little glue, and what was once garbage is now gorgeous. Twist them throughout loose, waved hair and watch them go from trash to flash in seconds flat.

You will need:

Trash twisties

Paint or pen (optional)

Good craft glue, such as Aleene's Tacky Glue

Flat-back rhinestones, beads, and glitter

1 If you like, color your trash twisties with paint or pen. Metallic pen looks especially nice. Allow ink to dry.

2 Glue on your rhinestones, beads, and glitter. Allow glue to set.

3 Twist into hair.

chinese

take-out tote

Aren't Chinese take-out cartons the most stylish food container there is? Next to drab Styrofoam containers and wax-paper bags, they're like beautiful little purses filled with chow fun. We think they're way too cute to ruin with egg-roll grease spots and soy sauce stains. Instead, transform one into a fashion-forward evening bag embellished with rhinestones and sparkly beads. It's just big enough for a lipstick, your keys, a few dollars, and a fortune cookie or two.

44

You will need:

Take-out carton (Ask your friendly Chinese restaurant for an extra one the next time you get take-out.)

Decorations: ribbon; flat-back rhinestones, pearls, beads, or gems; acrylic craft paint; glitter, sequins, rickrack, or whatever you like

Good craft glue, such as Aleene's Tacky Glue

Foam brush and glossy clear acrylic sealer (optional)

[1] First, you'll decorate the handle. The easiest way to do this is to wrap it with ribbon. You can spread a little glue on the handle and the back of the ribbon to keep it in place. Secure ends of ribbon with neat knots. Or, if you want to decorate the handle with big beads instead, you'll need to remove the handle from the carton. This looks really cool, but be warned: it can be tough to get the handle back in place, and it's easy to smush the carton, so proceed with caution. If you do decide to remove the handle, don't worry about getting it back in place until Step 4.

[2] Decorate your carton any way you like. Some ideas:
- Embellish the restaurant logo with tiny red rhinestones.
- Paint the whole carton to match your favorite outfit.
- Cover the whole carton with flat-back rhinestones, pearls, and beads.
- Glue on sequins in stripes or zigzags.
- Glue on a pretty ribbon or rickrack border.

continued on next page

[3] When decorations are set and dry, if you like, you can use your foam brush to give the whole carton a coat of glossy acrylic sealer for extra strength. Repeat for a stronger, shinier finish. Be sure to let it dry between coats, and be careful not to dislodge any decorations.

[4] If you've removed the handle, replace it now. You're all set! Now take *yourself* out, hot stuff.

glammy jammies

Just because you're not awake is no reason you can't look good. Adorn your pajamas with sequins, felt, flowers, ribbon, and other dreamy embellishments. You'll be the Sleeping Beauty of the slumber party—that is, if you ever stop talking and go to sleep.

You will need:

Pajamas (We like boy-style two-piece pj's best.)

Decorations: pearls, marabou boa, sequins, beads, felt cutouts, silk flowers, embroidery thread, ribbon, rickrack trim, or whatever you like (Bear in mind that you'll be sleeping in these, so avoid anything too big or bumpy.)

Needle and thread or washable fabric glue

continued on next page

[1] Get your goods and go to it. Give those pj's pizzazz.
Some ideas:
- Stitch pearls along the pockets, pants hem, sleeve cuffs, and collar.
- Sew or glue fluffy marabou boa to sleeve cuffs.
- Sew or glue sequins down the sides of the sleeves and pant legs, Elvis-style.
- Stitch on a sprinkling of beads.
- Sew or glue on felt cutouts of the moon and stars, hearts, flowers, or whatever you like. Use the stencils at the back of the book.
- Embroider your monogram, butterflies, little flowers, vines, or whatever you like.
- Sew on silk flowers or little ribbon rosettes.
- Add a border of ribbon or rickrack trim to pants hem and sleeve cuffs.

[2] Take a well-deserved nap.

Note   You'll want to hand wash and line dry your
Glammy Jammies to make sure you don't dislodge
any decorations in the machine. And if you sew
on marabou boa, consider them dry-clean only.
Just as well. A glamour-puss like yourself
doesn't have time for laundry, anyway.

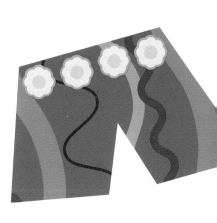

fantasy slippers

Your feet get jealous when the rest of your body gets to wear beads and ribbons and they don't. Make it up to them with these prima ballerina beauties. Ribbon laces make your Chinese slippers extra fancy and keep them from slipping off your feet.

You will need:

4 lengths of satin ribbon, each 1 yard long

Clear nail polish

Beaded Chinese slippers (available at your local Chinatown or import shops)

Tape

Needle and thread

[1] Brush ends of satin ribbon with clear nail polish to prevent fraying.

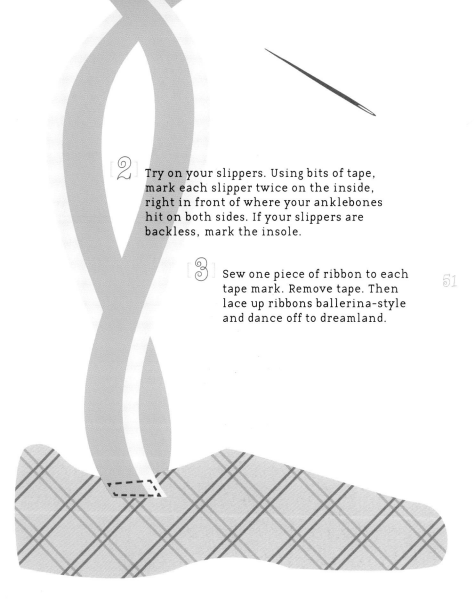

[2] Try on your slippers. Using bits of tape, mark each slipper twice on the inside, right in front of where your anklebones hit on both sides. If your slippers are backless, mark the insole.

[3] Sew one piece of ribbon to each tape mark. Remove tape. Then lace up ribbons ballerina-style and dance off to dreamland.

tinkerbell
slippers

You will need:

Copy machine or paper

Scissors

Straight pins

⅜ yard fleece

Needle and thread or sewing machine

Two pom-poms

First, you'll need to make your pattern. On a copy machine, enlarge diagram A until it fits your foot and cut out. Or, place your foot on a large piece of paper and use diagram A as a guide to draw and cut out the pattern. It doesn't have to be perfect, just try to keep the proportions about the same. Folding the paper in half lengthwise will help you cut more evenly.

[2] Pin pattern to fleece and cut out. Remove Pattern.

[3] Fold fleece in half as shown, with right-sides facing. Pin in place. Sew as shown in diagram B leaving a 1/2-inch seam allowance all around. Remove pins and turn right-side out. Repeat steps 2 and 3 to make other slipper.

[4] Sew a pom-pom onto the tip of each toe. Poof! Footwear magic.

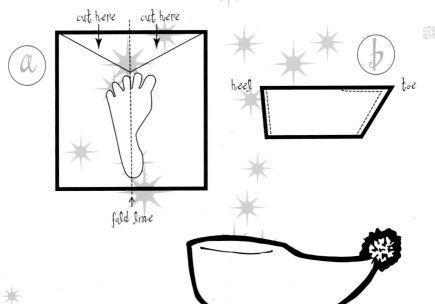

cut here   cut here

(a)

fold line

heel

toe

(b)

bombay bag

You will need:

2 pieces of Indian silk, 8 inches square (Look for a pretty, elaborate print. You could also use scarves or an old sari.)

Straight pins

Needle and thread or sewing machine

4 feet of silk cord

Clear nail polish

Decoration: exotic ribbon or trim, big unusual beads (optional)

1 On one side of a square of silk, fold one inch over on wrong side. Pin fold in place and stitch down. Repeat with other square of silk. Remove pins.

[2] Pin squares together with right sides facing each other. The edges you've just hemmed should be at the top. Sew sides and bottom together, leaving 1/2-inch seam allowances. Remove pins and turn right-side out.

[3] Brush ends of silk cord with nail polish to prevent fraying. Pin cord to the inside of your purse, about 1 inch down on each side, where side seams are. Sew in place.

[4] If you like, you can decorate for extra exoticism. Stitch on a border of beautiful ribbon or trim. Sew some big unusual beads along the bottom, 1 inch apart, for a quick fringe.

part 3

poolside panache

sarong

There's a warm wind on your face and a flower behind your ear, and you've got nothing to wear. Despair not, my Tahiti Sweetie. Whip up this easy breezy wrap to wear as a cover-up or a skirt. It's a sarong and it feels saright.

You will need:

1¾ yards fabric (lightweight cottons and rayons are best)

Pinking shears (optional)

Straight pins

Needle and thread or sewing machine

[1] If you want to avoid sewing at all costs, cut the raw edges of your fabric with pinking shears to prevent fraying, and skip to Step 4. Otherwise, go straight to Step 2.

[2] Fold 1/2-inch seam allowance under along raw edges and pin in place.

[3] Stitch seam allowance down with needle and thread or sewing machine. Remove pins.

[4] Wrap your instant Crafty Creation around your waist and knot the two top corners at your hip.

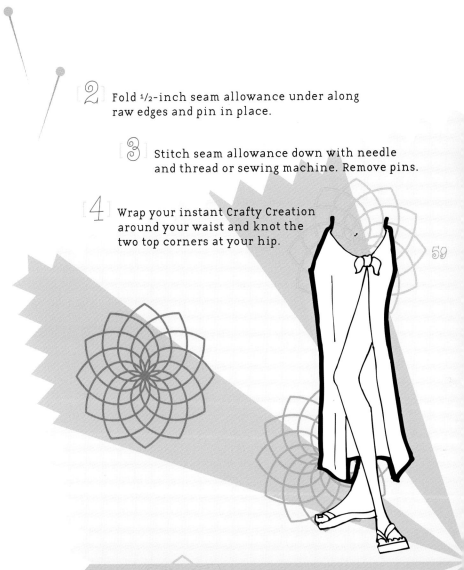

Souvenearrings

You may not always have Paris, but you'll always have the tacky plastic Eiffel Tower key chains you bought there. Transform souvenir key chains into wacky earrings. They're a great conversation piece and sooo jet set.

You will need:

2 souvenir key chains (Light plastic ones are best. Stay away from bronze medallions unless you want your lobes to look like Great-Aunty Zelda's.)

Round-nose pliers (Optional. Also known as needle-nose pliers, this little jewelry tool bends but doesn't crimp or cut wire, and is available at craft and bead stores.)

2 earring findings (The hook part that goes through your ear, available at craft and bead stores.)

2 jump rings (Plain little circle rings used to connect chain, available at craft and bead stores.)

[1] Remove key ring from each key chain, leaving just the ornament and the chain. Round-nose pliers might make this easier.

[2] Secure key chain to earring finding with a jump ring. Use pliers to close jump ring firmly. If you don't have pliers, you can just pinch really hard with your fingers. Repeat with other key chain and earring finding.

carmen miranda
barrettes

We love the frilly halter top, the saucy skirt, and the platform shoes. But the basket of fruit on your head is a little much. These fresh and fruity hair clips take a subtler route to the South American Way. Olé!

You will need:

Good craft glue, such as Aleene's Tacky Glue

Miniature fruit beads

2 plain metal barrettes (available at craft and bead stores)

Seed beads, rhinestones, or sequins (optional)

Beading needle and thread (optional)

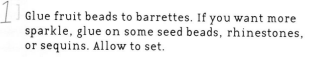

[1] Glue fruit beads to barrettes. If you want more sparkle, glue on some seed beads, rhinestones, or sequins. Allow to set.

[2] If your barrettes still don't seem fruity
enough, garnish with some fruit fringe.
Thread a few fruit beads and seed beads
onto your beading needle and thread.
Attach to barrette. Knot securely and snip
away excess thread.

lady of spain
floral fastener

Lady of Spain, we adore you. And we just love that gorgeous, great big silk rose in your hair. It makes us think of Majorca mamacitas sunning themselves on a Spanish beach. Muy bonita, chica!

You will need:

Needle and thread

Silk flower with the stem cut off (the bigger, the better)

Ponytail holder (the big thick kind)

[1] This project is *muy fácil*. Just stitch your flower to ponytail holder to secure. Knot securely and snip away excess thread.

[2] Wrap your Crafty Creation around your ponytail and go catch some rays. Don't forget the sunscreen. Crafty Girls know healthy skin is priority *número uno*.

read-all-over
beach tote

You can't stuff that juicy beach-reading paperback in just any old tote. Here's one that's worth a thousand words. Made from laminated magazine pages, it's quite a conversation piece. Read all about it!

You will need:

5 stylish magazine pages

Scissors

Clear contact paper

Hole punch

Ruler

32 ½-inch black rubber grommets (little rubber snaps, available at hardware stores. Note: you want grommets that are ½ inch in diameter at the widest outer circle part. The inner circle part is much smaller.)

4 yards clear plastic tubing, ⅛ inch in diameter (available at hardware stores)

Superglue

continued on next page

[1] First, trim the magazine pages to the appropriate sizes. You'll need two 8-by-10-inch pieces (the front and back), two 4-by-10-inch pieces (the sides), and one 4-by-8-inch piece (the bottom).

[2] Carefully lay these five pieces, picture-side down, on a sheet of contact paper as shown in diagram A, edges nearly touching, with the bottom piece in the middle as if you'd just cut open a paper bag. Place another sheet of contact paper on top and smooth out to seal. Trim away excess contact paper, so you end up with something that looks like a blocky laminated cross.

[3] Using your hole punch, starting exactly 1/4-inch from the bottom, make holes at 1-inch intervals along the left and right edges of the front, back, and side panels. Snap grommets into the holes you just made.

a

8 x 10

4 x 10   4 x 8   4 x 10

8 x 10

4   Cut 28 pieces of plastic tubing, each 3 inches long. Thread one of these pieces through the bottom holes of a side and front panel and tie in a knot. Snip away excess tubing. Continue with the rest of the pieces and the rest of the holes until the entire bag is sewn together.

5   Punch two more holes on both the front and back of the tote for the handle, as shown in diagram B. Snap grommets in holes. Then make your handles by threading a 2-foot piece of tubing through each set of holes you just made. Tie knots on the inside of the tote to secure handles. Dab a drop of superglue onto each of the knots for extra strength.

Crafty Girl

starlet sparkle
shades

You're a Crafty Superstar, and plain-Jane glasses just won't do. Give an ordinary pair of sunglasses star power by gluing on flat-back rhinestones. They'll dazzle the paparazzi while shading your eyes from the flashbulbs' glare. Wear them the next time a late night at a premiere leaves you with dark circles under your eyes.

You will need:

Sunglasses

Flat-back rhinestones

Good craft glue, such as Aleene's Tacky Glue

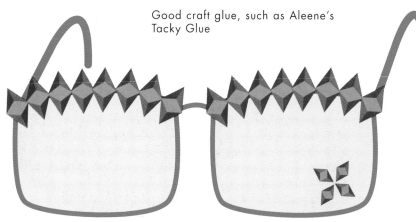

1. Make sure glasses are clean and dry. Then glue on your rhinestones. Some designs to try:
   - Glue rhinestones all over for a diamond-encrusted look.
   - Glue fifties-style flower patterns in the corners. Great for cat's-eye glasses.
   - Space rhinestones around the rims in a polka-dot pattern.
   - For big '70s-style glasses with no frames, you can glue rhinestones right on the glass, in the corner where they won't obscure your vision. Try making a butterfly or a heart out of really tiny rhinestones. Or monogram the lenses with your initials.

2. Allow glue to set. Then slip on your shades and go incognito, crafty girl.

flip-flop
fantasia

Dress up drab flip-flops with flashy embellishments. Put some spring in your step with silk flowers. Add some color with craft foam cutouts. Make them sparkle with flat-back rhinestones. Or transform them into glamorous mules with bits of marabou boa. A Crafty Girl is always on her toes.

You will need:

Hot-glue gun and an adult to supervise or good craft glue, such as Aleene's Tacky Glue

Decorations: marabou boa, plastic or silk flowers with the stems cut off (big flat ones, like daisies, work best), flat-back rhinestones, craft foam cutouts (cut hearts, flowers, moon and stars, sun and clouds, or whatever you like)

Flip-flops

1 Glue your boa, your flowers, your rhinestones, or your craft foam cutouts to your flip-flops.

2 Allow to set.

rosy posy
mary janes

Okay, so maybe your feet don't smell like roses. They can still look like roses. Decorated with fabulous flowers, these party shoes dance rings around plain Mary Janes. Ashes, ashes, we all fall down.

You will need:

2 big silk roses

Canvas Mary Jane–style shoes (available in your local Chinatown or import shop)

Needle and thread

6 small silk roses (optional)

1 Center a big silk rose on the toe of your shoe. Sew in place with needle and thread. If you like, you can sew a small silk rose on either side of the larger one and another small rose on the strap, near the buckle. Knot securely and snip off excess thread.

2 Repeat on other shoe.

part 4

class act
school stuff

yearbook beads

Your yearbook is one of your most treasured possessions. Pep rallies, funny faces, food fights: It's a record of it all. Ahhh, good times. If only you could wear it. Now you can. Transform your friends' class pictures into pendants. BFF! KIT! CAT! (Best Friends Forever, Keep in Touch, Call Anytime. But you already knew that.)

You will need:

Picture of your favorite person

Color copier, or scanner and color printer

Scissors

Glue stick

Cabochon setting, ½ inch in diameter (A cabochon is simply an empty jewelry setting, available at craft and bead stores. Look for a pendant setting or, if you're really lucky, a bracelet or necklace setting with several cabochons linked together.)

Adhesive-backed, clear plastic furniture bumper, ½ inch in diameter (These are the little thingies Mom uses to keep the chairs from scraping the hardwood floors, and you can find them in any hardware store.)

[1] First, make a copy of your picture, 1/2 inch in diameter, using a color copier or a scanner and a color printer. Cut this copy into a circle.

[2] Glue your picture to your cabochon setting. Allow glue to set.

[3] Peel backing off furniture bumper and stick on top of the picture. That's it! Link several settings together and you can turn your most charming classmates into a charm bracelet.

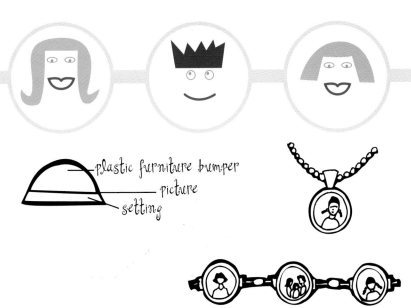

plastic furniture bumper
picture
setting

pearl-drop choker

Shall I compare this necklace to a summer's day? It is more lovely, and more temperate, and much more crafty. It's as darling as the buds of May, and we think Shakespeare would have fallen in love with it. We can just picture it around Juliet's throat. And if it doesn't get you an A in English, you'll still get high marks for fashion.

You will need:

56 faux pearls in assorted sizes

56 gold head pins (A straight, plain pin with a little base at the end to hold on the beads, available at craft and bead stores.)

16-inch gold chain with clasp

Round-nose pliers (Optional. Also known as needle-nose pliers, this little jewelry tool bends but doesn't crimp or cut wire, and is available at craft and bead stores.)

Wire cutters and an adult to supervise

[1] Place a pearl onto a head pin. Thread this head pin through a link in your gold chain, about an inch down from the clasp. Bend pin back and twist around several times to secure as pictured. Jewelry pliers might make this easier, but you can also use your fingers. Snip away the excess part of the pin with wire cutters.

[2] Repeat with the rest of the pearls, spacing them 1/4 inch apart.

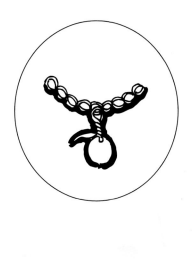

daywear tiara

You're a princess and you deserve royal treatment. But the crown jewels are a little much for homeroom, and Buckingham Palace is awfully touchy about lending them out. Make a sparkler that's subtle enough for school instead. This one is informal enough for weekday wear but still will let you feel like a queen.

You will need:

Wire cutters and an adult to supervise

28-gauge wire

Wire rake headband

Clear seed beads

An assortment of small, medium, and large clear crystal beads

1 Cut a yard or so of wire. Secure wire to first tooth of headband by wrapping it around tooth several times.

2 String on a seed bead, a small crystal, and another seed bead. Loop around next tooth. Repeat on the third and fourth teeth.

3 On the fifth tooth, string on a seed bead, a small crystal, and three seed beads. Pass wire back through small crystal and add another seed bead. Loop around next tooth. Repeat pattern in Step 2.

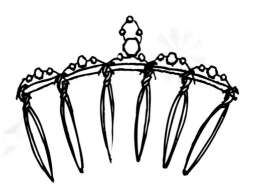

continued on next page

[4] On every fifth tooth, repeat pattern in Step 3.
Graduate crystal size, so as you approach the
middle of the headband, you're using medium
crystals; at the middle, you're using large ones;
and as you work your way toward the other end,
you're using medium and then small ones
again; see illustration on page 79. If you run out
of wire, secure end by wrapping it around a
tooth several times, and then start a new
length of wire the same way.

[5] When you reach the end of the
headband, secure wire around last tooth.
Cut away excess wire.

[6] Don your tiara and command a loyal
subject to bring you a chocolate milk.

picture platforms

Maybe you're craving some color. Maybe you think your feet need a little more attention. Or maybe you just want a certain someone's face under your heel. We're sure you've got a good reason to make these extraordinary platform shoes. Covered with pictures of your favorite faces, this pair is one of a kind.

You will need:

Découpage medium, like Mod Podge or Ceramcoat brand

Pictures

Platform shoes (preferably with a smooth, porous heel, like cork)

Stickers, flat-back gems, glitter, or whatever you like

Good craft glue, such as Aleene's Tacky Glue

Foam brush

Glossy clear acrylic sealer (optional)

continued on next page

[1] Brush a little découpage medium on the backs of your pictures and stick them to the heels of your shoes wherever you want them.

[2] Embellish by adding stickers or by gluing on gems, glitter, or whatever you like. Allow to set.

[3] Using your foam brush, brush on a coat of découpage medium. Watch out for air bubbles and wrinkles in the pictures. Allow to dry. Repeat until you're satisfied.

[4] For extra shine and strength, add a coat or two of glossy clear acrylic sealer. Allow to dry.

fuzzy logic

purse

It's simple: fur + purse = Crafty Fashion fun. This little creation is easier than algebra, and it's sure to make you look smart. Add it up!

You will need:

2 pieces of fun fur, 6 inches square

Straight pins

1 strip of fun fur, 4 by 14 inches

Needle and thread

 On one side of a fun-fur square, fold one inch over, wrong-sides facing. Pin fold in place and stitch down. Remove pins. Repeat with other square of fun fur.

[2] Pin squares together, right-sides facing. The edges you've just hemmed should be at the top. Sew sides and bottom together, leaving a 1/2-inch seam allowance. Unpin and turn right-side out.

[3] All you need to do now is make the strap. Fold your 4-by-14-inch strip of fun fur in half lengthwise, right-sides facing. Pin together. Sew along cut edge, leaving half-inch seam allowance, to make a tube. Unpin and turn inside out. Trimming the seam allowance may make this easier.

[4] Pin your strap to the inside of your purse, about 1 inch down on each side. Sew in place.

fashion emergency
survival kit

We've all done it: arrived at school, looked down at what we were wearing, and realized we'd made a horrible, horrible mistake. Can't go home to change? This kit uses your Crafty Ingenuity to transform a fashion tragedy into a future fashion trend. Keep your survival kit in your locker, and the next time you get dressed in the dark, you'll still be able to see the light at the end of the tunnel.

You will need:

An adorable little bag

Safety pins

Large rhinestone brooch

Heart-shaped patch

White T-shirt

Pink scarf

Starlet Sparkle Shades (page 68)

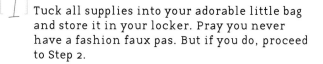

[1] Tuck all supplies into your adorable little bag and store it in your locker. Pray you never have a fashion faux pas. But if you do, proceed to Step 2.

[2] First, you must diagnose what your emergency is. Fashion emergencies tend to fall into four categories:

- **Rips:** The solution? Safety pins. They're the perfect quick fix for a broken halter strap, a split pants seam, or a fallen hem.

- **Stains:** Yes, you could try to get it out with a little water. But we don't recommend it. The only thing worse than a stain on your butt is a great big wet patch on your butt. Conceal stains above your waist by pinning a large rhinestone brooch over them. Below your waist, use a heart-shaped patch and a safety pin.

- **Color crisis:** Sure, red and magenta looked fine together in the dim light of your bedroom, but now, in the fluorescent glare of the classroom, you're making your classmates' eyeballs bleed. If you've got a spare white T-shirt in your locker, throw that on instead. If not, your only hope is to draw their eyes elsewhere. Tie a pretty pink scarf around your neck so you'll have a flattering color near your face, and pray they don't look down. If it's not too warm, wear your coat all day.

continued on next page

- **The fashion risk that fails:** It looked great in the magazine, but it doesn't look so hot in home-room. You want to spend the day hiding in your locker. But if you were brave enough to pair Bermuda shorts with a fun-fur bikini top, you're brave enough to survive this day. Your first sur-vival strategy: confidence. Throw your shoulders back and make a face that says, "I meant to wear this." If you're successful, everyone will come to school in neon green Bermuda shorts and fun-fur bikini tops the next day. If you're not, you have one more option. Put on your Starlet Sparkle Shades (page 68), tie your scarf around your head, and go incognito. You may want to affect a sophisticated accent. This is a technique best used by Drama Club members, who can simply claim to be "in character."

[3] Put it behind you and move on. Tomorrow someone will wear something even worse than what you wore today, and The Great Bermuda Shorts Fiasco will fade from every-one's memory—even yours.

locker lounge

Okay, so you can't wear it, but how you decorate your locker says something about how crafty a girl you are. It's the only space at school that's yours, all yours. Think of it as a really tiny lounge. If only it were big enough for a blender and smoothie supplies. It isn't, but it should still be more than a dank, dark crypt for your books and gym clothes. Here are some ideas to make it look its best.

You will need:

Fun fur

Heavy-duty double-stick adhesive

Wrapping paper

Scotch tape

Key chain–size disco mirror ball

Pictures, stickers, and mementos

Craft foam

Good craft glue, such as Aleene's Tacky Glue

Magnet-backed Lucite frame

Magnet-backed mirror

Refreshments

Beauty supplies

continued on next page

[1] First, you'll want to make your locker look its best. If you're really ambitious, you can line the whole thing with fun fur, using heavy-duty double-stick adhesive to attach the fur to the locker walls. You could also line it with fancy wrapping paper using Scotch tape. Attach a key chain–size disco mirror ball to the ceiling.

[2] Next, you'll add some personal touches. Put up pictures, stickers, mementos. You can make a special locker picture frame by cutting a funky frame shape out of craft foam and gluing it to a magnet-backed Lucite frame. Now for the most personal touch of all: a mirror, so you can get an eyeful of your lovely self between each class.

[3] Finally, you'll stock your locker lounge with get-you-through-the-day goodies: refreshments and beauty supplies, mood-reviving elixirs like essential oils and potpourri, or whatever gets you going. Between algebra and history you can treat yourself to a five-minute mini-spa. Ahhhhh.

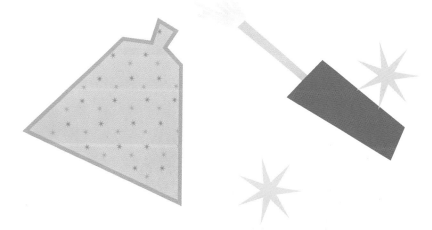

bohemian

backpack

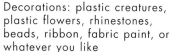

Milky Pen graffiti and beaded safety pins are decoration enough for some folks, but a Crafty Girl like you turns her backpack into a true showpiece, worthy of a trek across Europe and the Himalayas. Seems a shame to wear it on your back, where you can't see it. Well, everyone else will enjoy it. Here are some ideas to get you started.

You will need:

Backpack

Decorations: plastic creatures, plastic flowers, rhinestones, beads, ribbon, fabric paint, or whatever you like

Assorted supplies: needle and thread, fabric glue, stencils at back of book, or whatever will get the job done

[1] Get your goods and go to town. Some ideas:

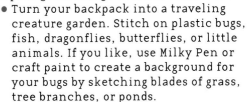

- Turn your backpack into a traveling creature garden. Stitch on plastic bugs, fish, dragonflies, butterflies, or little animals. If you like, use Milky Pen or craft paint to create a background for your bugs by sketching blades of grass, tree branches, or ponds.

- Give your pack some flower power. Cut the stems off plastic or silk flowers (big, flat flowers like daisies work best), and stitch to your pack.

- Use fabric glue to dot flat-back rhinestones, pearls, and beads all over.

- Sew on an assortment of buttons in all colors and sizes.

- Make it a snack pack. Glue or stitch on little plastic hamburgers and candies. Paint on ice cream cones or pizza slices.

- Stitch on rickrack, ribbon, or pom-pom trim.

- If you're *really* crafty and you've got some time on your hands, embroider a design. Stitch on your name, favorite flowers, ladybugs, or whatever you like.

[2] Strap on your back and hit the trail, Crafty Girl-style.

fancy

folders

folders

Dull Pee-Chees? Not for you, Crafty Girl. Dress up dreary folders with a collage of color. You'll get an A+ for style.

You will need any or all of the following:

Folders

Mirrorflex (sheets of shiny little squares with adhesive backing, available at craft stores)

Contact paper (look in craft stores for fancy variations, like glitter, fractals, or 3-D)

Good craft glue, such as Aleene's Tacky Glue

Felt

Rickrack trim

Ribbon

Fun fur

Googly eyes

Mini pom-poms

Craft foam

Ribbon roses

Pictures

Paper glue

Sequins

Glitter

Beads

Rhinestones

[1] Get your goods and go for it. Some ideas:

- **Disco Inferno Folder:** Decorate a folder with Mirrorflex. Cover the whole thing with a sheet of the stuff, or break up the little squares and make patterns. It looks especially cool with a few squares sprinkled at the top and more as you go down, like snowflakes.

- **Freaky Fractals Folder:** Cover with fractal-patterned contact paper.

- **Felt Folder:** Cover with felt. Then glue on felt cutouts of faces, flowers, hearts, stars, or whatever you like. Add ribbon or rickrack trim.

- **Fuzzy Folder:** Cover in fun fur. If you like, add googly eyes and a pom-pom nose.

continued on next page

- **Foamy Folder:** Decorate with craft foam cutouts in any shape you like. Layer stacks of foam in different colors for a 3-D effect. Use stencils at back of book.

- **Flower Folder:** Glue on little ribbon roses.

- **Teen Idol Altar Folder:** Glue a picture of your fave rave to the center of your folder with paper glue. Surround the portrait with pictures of roses cut from magazines or flower stickers, and add sequins and expressions of love. Cover the whole thing with clear contact paper to keep your precious one clean and safe.

- **Sparkle Folder:** Cover folder with sequins, beads, and rhinestones.

- **Collage Folder:** Cover folder with pictures and phrases cut from magazines. Then cover the whole thing with clear contact paper.

- **Frame Folder:** Make a frame from craft foam and glue three sides of frame to your folder, leaving one side open so you can slip in a photo of your favorite person.

- **School Spirit Folder:** Cover the whole surface with mini pom-poms in your school colors.

[2] Allow glue to set. You've done your Crafty Homework, all right.

English

part 5

on-the-go gear

rapid wraps

When it's cold outside, you just want to be a human burrito, all wrapped up in a fleece tortilla. Now you can make yourself a cozy wrap in less time than it takes to hit the Taco Bell drive-thru. Use any fabric you like. For a casual, sporty wrap, use fleece. For an industrial-strength one, use boiled wool. Brocade makes a gypsy princess shawl. Sheer fabric makes a fairy queen one. You've got Crafty Fashion all wrapped up.

You will need:

1 ¼ yards fabric (You can use almost anything that's about 45 inches wide, but you'll want to avoid knits, which are hard to sew and not that cute anyway.)

Scissors

Pinking shears (optional)

Straight pins

Needle and thread or sewing machine

4 ½ yards pretty trim, ribbon, lace, rickrack, or whatever you want to decorate with (optional)

Beads, rhinestones, or pearls (optional)

[1] Lay your fabric out on a table or the floor. Cut a diagonal from the bottom left corner to the top right corner. You'll end up with two triangles, each about 45 by 45 by 64 inches. Set one triangle aside to make a shawl for a friend later.

[2] If you shudder at the thought of sewing, cut along the edges of your triangle with pinking shears. This will prevent fraying. Otherwise, turn edges 1/2 inch under, secure with straight pins, sew in place with a needle and thread or sewing machine, and unpin. If you're using fleece or boiled wool, you can skip this step because your fabric won't fray.

[3] If your shawl wants some embellishment, pin your trim, ribbon, lace, or rickrack in place with straight pins. Sew down with needle and thread or a sewing machine. Or stitch on a few beads for extra sparkle.

thing rings

Sure, diamonds are a girl's best friend, but Crafty Girls prefer something a little more colorful. We like these unique Thing Rings. Glue pom-poms or plastic creatures onto ring blanks for a fistful of fun.

You will need:

Good craft glue, such as Aleene's Tacky Glue

Mini pom-pom, plastic bug, plastic sushi, plastic flower, or any other little creature you like

Ring blank (available at craft and bead stores)

1 Glue pom-pom or creature onto ring blank.

2 Allow to set. Then make nine more and transform your hands into a plastic creature zoo.

feathery
fastener

Scrunchies are okay for gym class, but there are times you want your ponytail to be a little more polished. Make this fancy feathered fastener instead. It's instant updo glamour.

You will need:

Marabou boa, cut just half as long as the circumference of your ponytail holder

Ponytail holder (The simpler, the better. You want a plain nylon-covered rubber band—the big thick kind works best.)

Straight pins

Needle and thread

1 Secure boa to half of ponytail holder with straight pins.

2 Stitch down, then knot off securely. Snip away excess thread.

3 Arrange in hair so boa strip is facing out.

milkmaid

kerchief

With cows to milk and chickens to feed, you don't have much time for crafting. Good thing you can whip up this country-fresh head scarf in a New York minute—no sewing required. It'll keep the hay out of your hair in high style. Looking good's no chore.

You will need:

Pinking shears

Swatch of gingham or other fabric

1 yard rickrack trim or ribbon

Fabric glue

[1] Use pinking shears to cut a triangle of fabric, about 12 by 12 by 16 inches.

[2] Glue rickrack trim or ribbon along long side of triangle and let it extend 10 inches on each side to tie at the nape of your neck.

[3] That's it! Y'all come back, y'hear?

happy-go-lucky
messenger bag

You're on the go, and you've got to take it all with you. But your CD player, cell phone, pager, keys, lip gloss, protein bars, and wrench kit are really weighing down the pockets on your cargo pants. Store your gear in this easy, fleecy bag instead. Va-va-vroom.

You will need:

14-by-14-inch piece of polar fleece

14-by-22-inch piece of polar fleece

Straight pins

Sewing machine or needle and thread

4 inches of narrow ribbon or cord

Big button

4 feet of strap cord

Clear nail polish

Felt cutouts (optional)

1 Line up fleece pieces on three edges, right-sides facing, and pin together. Sew sides and bottom, leaving a 1-inch seam allowance. Leave top open. Unpin and turn right-side out. The longer piece of fleece should fold over.

continued on next page

[2] Fold the narrow ribbon or cord in half and sew the loop onto the edge of the fold-over fleece, right in the center. This will form your button-hole. Sew large button to fleece underneath.

[3] Brush ends of strap cord with clear nail polish to prevent fraying. Allow to dry. Then sew strap cord to back of bag, about 2 inches down and 1 inch in from the edges on each side. Stitch big X's to secure.

[4] For more color, you can sew on felt cutouts of hearts, stars, letters, or whatever you like.

chic sneaks

Now you can work it while you work out. Glam up your gym shoes with sequins, beads, or rhinestones. Look hot without even breaking a sweat.

You will need:

Canvas sneakers

Decorations: sequins, beads, flat-back rhinestones, pearls, puffy paint, ribbon rosettes, googly eyes, mini pom-poms, or whatever you like

Hot-glue gun and an adult to supervise, good fabric glue, or needle and thread

Fancy shoelaces or ribbon (optional)

continued on next page

[1] Make sure shoes are clean and dry. Then get your goods and go wild. Some designs to try:

- Cover every inch of your shoes with sequins, beads, or rhinestones for over-the-top sparkle.
- Glue on pearl polka dots.
- Make flowers or faces out of beads, sequins, or puffy paint.
- Make stripes and zigzags out of beads, sequins, or puffy paint.
- Glue or stitch on tiny ribbon rosettes.
- Make a face on the toe by gluing on googly eyes and a pom-pom nose.

2 Allow glue to set.

3 If you want, replace boring laces with fancy printed ones or pretty ribbons. Then go for a fashionable little run.

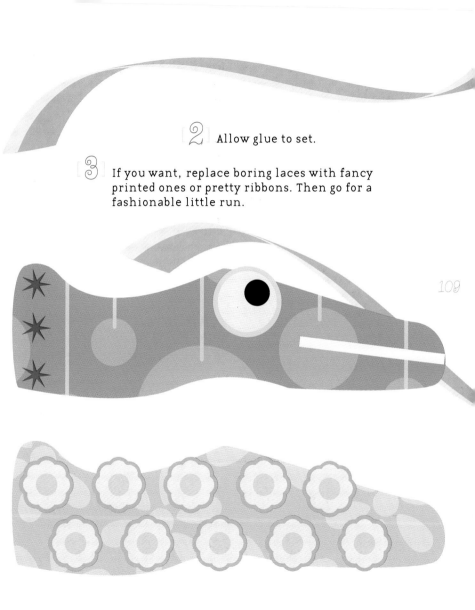

fun-fur

pager cozy

You can't let your pager go around naked. Make it this stylish jacket instead. It'll stay safe and warm when it's not glued to your hip. Make a matching coat for your Walkman, and you'll have the best-dressed electronic equipment on the block.

You will need:

3½-by-7-inch piece of fun fur

Straight pins

Needle and thread

Sew-on snap

4 feet of cord or lightweight chain (optional)

[1] Fold fun fur as pictured in diagram A, with right-sides facing and 1¹/₂ inches free at top. Pin in place.

[2] Sew sides with needle and thread, leaving a ¹/₄-inch seam allowance, and unpin.

[3] Turn right-side out. Sew snap to front.

[4] If you like, you can add a strap of cord or lightweight chain. Pin cord or chain to the inside of your cozy, about 1 inch down on each side, where side seams are. Sew in place as shown in diagram B.

[5] Call a friend and tell her all about your adorable Crafty Creation.

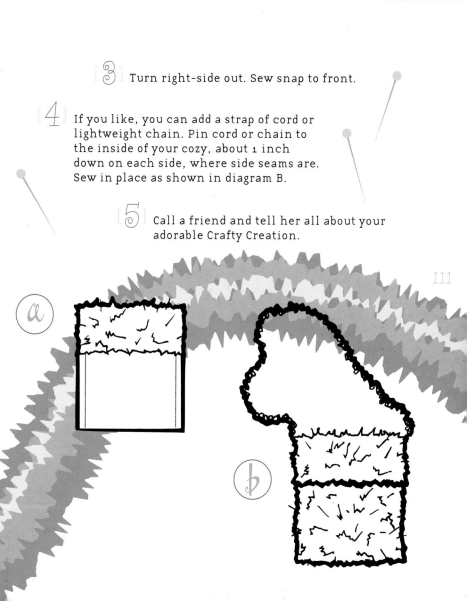

the end